Materials

written by Maria Gordon
and
illustrated by Mike Gordon

Wayland

Simple Science

Air	Light
Colour	Materials
Day and Night	Push and Pull
Electricity and Magnetism	Rocks and Soil
Float and Sink	Skeletons and Movement
Heat	Sound

Series Editor: Catherine Baxter
Advice given by Audrey Randall – member of the Science Working Group for the National Curriculum.

First published in 1996 by
Wayland (Publishers) Ltd
61 Western Road, Hove
East Sussex, BN3 1JD, England

British Library Cataloguing in Publication Data
Gordon, Maria
  Materials. – (Simple Science Series)
  I. Title II. Gordon, Mike III. Series
  535.6

ISBN 0-7502-1601-8

Typeset by MacGuru
Printed and bound in Italy by G. Canale and C.S.p.A., Turin, Italy

Contents

Touch and look at some things around you. They are made of different things. The things they are made of are called materials.

Metal, wood and cotton are materials.
Can you find...

a saucepan made
of metal,

a table made of wood,

a T-shirt made
of cotton.

A metal saucepan feels hard. It doesn't burn.
A wooden table feels hard. It holds things up.
A cotton T-shirt is soft. It is comfortable and
it keeps you warm.

Different materials are good
for different things.

Would you like
to wear a metal
T-shirt...

or cook with a
wooden
saucepan?

Cave people made arrowheads and axes from stones. They used clay to make pots, and powder from rocks to make paint. Huts were built with mud and plants.

People learnt to weave leaves and stems to make baskets, ropes and nets. More and more materials were used to make different things. Which things can you see here? What are they made of?

Pour some water.

Watch it spread out.

Put your finger in it.

Now pull it out.

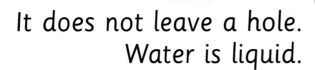

It does not leave a hole.
Water is liquid.

If you put a stone
into a cup, it does
not spread out.

But if something
makes a hole in a
stone, the hole does
not go away.
Stones are solid.

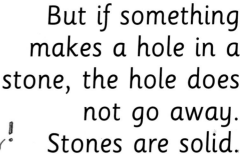

Half fill a plastic bag with water.

The water stays in the bottom of the bag.

Blow up another bag. The air does not stay at the bottom. It fills the bag.

Air is a gas. All materials are solids, liquids or gases.

Gases can be useful materials. If you whip air into cream, it makes it frothy.

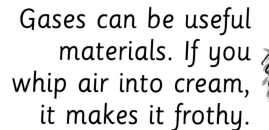

Gas from yeast makes bread rise.

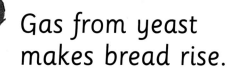

If you switch on a light with a tube-shaped bulb, gas inside the tube glows and helps you to see.

Many solids are useful materials. They keep their shape and size.

You can build with solid building blocks. They don't float up in the air! They don't mix with the floor! Tables don't spread out and fill the room and paper doesn't pour away!

Liquids often mix with other materials. Add water to sand. The water makes the sand stiff. Now you can make sandcastles.

You can make things by mixing solids, liquids and gases together. Ask a grown-up to help you make a milkshake. Use...

250 ml of milk
250 ml of vanilla ice-cream
2 sliced bananas
2 cartons of strawberries.

Wash and top the strawberries.
Put all the solids and the milk into a blender.
Switch it on and watch air mix in and froth up your shake!

Look for solid
liquid and gas materials.

What do these materials look like?
What colour are they?
What do they feel like?

Touch a new
piece of silver
foil. It is hard
and smooth.
It looks shiny.

Look at sand. It is
made of tiny,
hard pieces.
It feels gritty.

Pour some flour.
It is made of even tinier pieces.
It is very soft.

Feel some wool.
It is soft and light.
What colour is it?

Touch some honey. Is it soft and runny or lumpy and stiff?

YUM, YUM!

17

Materials can change when you do things to them. Crumple some silver foil. Now it feels rough.

Pour water from high up. Watch it move fast. Bend and twist some Plasticine. Feel it go soft.

18

Ask a grown-up to help you.

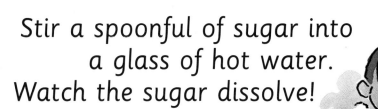

Stir a spoonful of sugar into
a glass of hot water.
Watch the sugar dissolve!

Watch the liquid in a
thermometer go up
when it gets hot.

Heat ice cubes in a saucepan. Watch them
change into water. Heat the water until it
bubbles. Watch the water change into steam.
Changing materials makes them useful for
different things.

Materials come from the world around us.
Wood comes from trees.
Stones and oil come from rocks.

Rubber and cotton come from plants.

Wool and leather come from animals.

Brush a pet.
How could you
use the fur?

These sorts of
materials are called
natural materials.

J620·11

21

Some natural materials can be mixed to make new ones.

Add water to flour. This makes a sticky paste. Soak newspaper in the paste. It dries stiff and hard. This is papier mâché.

Scientists have learnt how to change natural materials.
They make new materials that are not found in the world around us.
These are artificial materials.

Look at a bendy doll and a telephone. Today, these are made of plastic.

Feel a pair of stockings. These are made of nylon. Nylon and plastic are artificial materials.

Some things make materials change. Find a rusty nail. The nail is made of iron but it has mixed with air and water and made rust. Feel an old tree stump. Rain can make wood soft and crumbly. Look at bricks in a wall. Wind and rain can wear away the cement in between the bricks.

Some animals and insects can make materials.

Bees make honey and wax

Silkworms make silk.

Wasps chew up wood and plants to make papery nests.

What materials were used to build your house? Why were they used?
Would you make windows out of clingfilm or glass? Why?
Would you make a roof out of cardboard or tiles? Why?
Would you make doors out of stone or wood? Why?

Over the years, people have used different kinds of materials to build houses. Different materials are used in different countries too. In hot countries windows can be holes. In cold ones, glass makes strong, clear windows. Roofs can be giant leaves that keep out rain, but tiles last longer. Stone doors are very heavy. Wood is easier to cut and use.

The world keeps on making materials.
It uses old ones to make new ones. This is
called recycling. Old trees and plants crumble
into soil. Soil helps grow new
trees and plants.

People must recycle too
because we are using up
materials faster than the
world is making them.

Look at the next
page.

What materials
can you see?
Which ones can
you recycle?

Notes for adults

The 'Simple Science' series helps children to reach Key Stage 1: Attainment Targets 1-4 of the Science National Curriculum.

Below are some suggestions to help complement and extend the learning in this book.

4/5   Compare materials such as cotton, plastic, metal and wood. Make bar charts of toys and classroom/kitchen items made from the materials. Compare materials in items of decoration and entertainment from jewellery to musical instruments.

6/7   Make 'boats' out of paper, lollysticks, food containers, bottlecaps, etc. Note materials involved. Predict which will sail the longest, farthest, etc. On a rainy day, test hats made from paper, foil, plastic, cloth, etc.

8/9   Visit museums. Try weaving. Play with clay. Investigate the travels and trade of Marco Polo and other explorers.

10/11   Pour, freeze and boil water. Talk about solids, liquids and gases in the immediate environment.

12/13   Demonstrate 'dry ice' fire extinguishers. Blow bubbles.

14/15   Make cakes. Watch cement being made. Use watercolours.

16/17   Sing songs like, 'Mud, Glorious Mud', 'A Spoonful of Honey' and 'Yellow Submarine'. Write a poem around a chosen quality (rough, sticky, etc.). Test materials for strength and insulation. Look at packaging. Make raw eggs bounce on their pointed ends.

18/19   Visit a foundry, a pottery, and glass works. Burn toast. Sand wood. Play 'Scissors, Paper, Rock'.

20/21   Display raw materials. Research their value. Plot countries of origin.

Investigate how Amazon peoples waterproofed their clothing and bodies with rubber plant sap, how Egyptians made paper from papyrus, etc. See how dandelion sap, a natural latex, dries. Burn the end of a cork to make charcoal for drawing or face painting. Visit shops and study food and clothing labels.

22/23 Make paper. Compare plastic and leather shoes and balls, and traditional and nylon fishing nets. Look at use of materials past and present, and in developed and undeveloped world.

24/25 Spot signs of weathering on buildings. Look at erosion of rocks and cliffs. Collect water-worn wood, glass, etc. – display and write stories about them. Observe spiders' webs, cocoons and slug slime. What inventions could these inspire?

26/27 Read 'The Three Little Pigs'. Write and perform new versions. Discuss materials used in own homes. Ask a surveyor to talk.

28/29 Make collages from scrap materials. Join recycling schemes. Start a compost heap. Visit a dump!

Other books to read

Bangles, Badges and Beads by C. Deshpande (A & C Black, 1990)
Materials by G. Peacock (Wayland, 1994)
Nuffield Primary Science: Materials (Harper Collins, 1993)
Wood and Paper (Ginn, 1990)

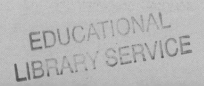

Index

air 11-13, 15, 24
animals 21, 25

bricks 24

cave people 8
clay 8
cotton 5-6, 21

gases 11-12, 15-16
glass 26-27

leather 21
leaves 9, 27
liquids 10-11, 14-16

metal 5-7
mud 8

nylon 23

paper 13
    newspaper 22
plants 8, 12, 25, 28
plastic 23

recycling 28-29
rust 24

sand 14, 16
shape 13
solids 10-13, 15-16

wood 5-7, 20, 24-27